50 Oregon State Recipes for Home

By: Kelly Johnson

Table of Contents

- Marionberry Pie
- Dungeness Crab Cakes
- Hazelnut Crusted Salmon
- Tillamook Cheese Soup
- Oregon Pinot Noir Braised Lamb Shanks
- Oregon Hazelnut Pesto Pasta
- Pacific Northwest Clam Chowder
- Oregon Blackberry Cobbler
- Grilled Oregon Coast Oysters
- Huckleberry Pancakes
- Wild Mushroom Risotto
- Marionberry BBQ Sauce
- Oregon Trail Mix
- Rogue River Blue Cheese Salad
- Hazelnut Crusted Chicken
- Tillamook Ice Cream Sundae
- Oregon Hazelnut Encrusted Halibut
- Marionberry Jam
- Oregon Pear Salad with Blue Cheese
- Grilled Columbia River Steelhead
- Hazelnut Butter Cookies
- Tillamook Cheesecake
- Oregon Coast Seafood Linguine
- Marionberry Muffins
- Hazelnut Crusted Pork Chops
- Tillamook Macaroni and Cheese
- Oregon Berry Smoothie
- Columbia River Salmon Salad
- Hazelnut Toffee
- Tillamook Cheeseburger
- Oregon Trail Mix Cookies
- Hazelnut Chocolate Bark
- Tillamook Cheese Fondue
- Oregon Berry Parfait
- Hazelnut Espresso Brownies

- Tillamook Yogurt Dip
- Oregon Pear and Hazelnut Salad
- Marionberry Sorbet
- Hazelnut Crusted Tilapia
- Tillamook Cheese Stuffed Mushrooms
- Oregon Berry Crisp
- Hazelnut Encrusted Brie
- Tillamook Cheese and Herb Bread
- Oregon Berry Pie
- Hazelnut Pancakes
- Tillamook Cheese Soup
- Oregon Berry Salsa
- Hazelnut Crusted Tofu
- Tillamook Ice Cream Sandwiches
- Oregon Berry Lemonade

Marionberry Pie

Ingredients:

For the crust:

- 2 ½ cups all-purpose flour
- 1 tablespoon granulated sugar
- 1 teaspoon salt
- 1 cup unsalted butter, cold and cut into small cubes
- ½ cup ice water

For the filling:

- 6 cups fresh Marionberries, rinsed and drained
- 1 cup granulated sugar
- ¼ cup cornstarch
- 1 tablespoon lemon juice
- 1 teaspoon lemon zest
- ½ teaspoon ground cinnamon
- Pinch of salt
- 2 tablespoons unsalted butter, cut into small pieces

For egg wash (optional):

- 1 egg
- 1 tablespoon water

Instructions:

1. Prepare the crust:
    - In a large mixing bowl, combine the flour, sugar, and salt.
    - Add the cold cubed butter to the flour mixture. Using a pastry cutter or your fingertips, cut the butter into the flour until the mixture resembles coarse crumbs.
    - Gradually add the ice water, a little at a time, mixing until the dough comes together. Be careful not to overwork the dough.

- Divide the dough into two equal portions, shape each into a disk, wrap them in plastic wrap, and refrigerate for at least 1 hour.
2. Make the filling:
    - In a large bowl, gently toss the Marionberries with sugar, cornstarch, lemon juice, lemon zest, cinnamon, and salt until well combined. Let the mixture sit for about 15 minutes to allow the flavors to meld.
3. Preheat the oven:
    - Preheat your oven to 400°F (200°C).
4. Roll out the crust:
    - On a lightly floured surface, roll out one disk of the chilled dough into a circle large enough to line a 9-inch pie dish. Carefully transfer the dough to the pie dish, gently pressing it into the bottom and sides. Trim any excess dough hanging over the edges.
5. Fill the pie:
    - Pour the Marionberry filling into the prepared pie crust, spreading it out evenly. Dot the top of the filling with small pieces of butter.
6. Top the pie:
    - Roll out the second disk of dough into a circle large enough to cover the pie. You can leave it whole or cut it into strips for a lattice top. If using a whole crust, make several slits in the top to allow steam to escape during baking. If making a lattice, weave the strips over the filling.
7. Optional egg wash:
    - In a small bowl, whisk together the egg and water. Brush the top crust (or lattice) with the egg wash for a golden finish.
8. Bake the pie:
    - Place the pie on a baking sheet to catch any drips. Bake in the preheated oven for 45-50 minutes, or until the crust is golden brown and the filling is bubbling. If the edges of the crust start to brown too quickly, you can cover them with foil halfway through baking.
9. Cool and serve:
    - Allow the pie to cool on a wire rack for at least 1 hour before serving. Serve slices of Marionberry pie with a scoop of vanilla ice cream or a dollop of whipped cream, if desired.

Enjoy your delicious homemade Marionberry Pie!

Dungeness Crab Cakes

Ingredients:

- 1 pound Dungeness crab meat, picked over for shells
- 1 cup breadcrumbs (preferably Panko)
- 1/4 cup mayonnaise
- 2 green onions, finely chopped
- 1/4 cup red bell pepper, finely chopped
- 2 tablespoons fresh parsley, finely chopped
- 1 tablespoon Dijon mustard
- 1 large egg, lightly beaten
- 1 tablespoon Worcestershire sauce
- 1 tablespoon lemon juice
- 1/2 teaspoon Old Bay seasoning
- Salt and pepper to taste
- 1/4 cup all-purpose flour (for coating)
- 2 tablespoons butter
- 2 tablespoons olive oil
- Lemon wedges, for serving
- Tartar sauce or aioli, for serving (optional)

Instructions:

1. Prepare the crab mixture:
    - In a large mixing bowl, combine the Dungeness crab meat, breadcrumbs, mayonnaise, chopped green onions, red bell pepper, parsley, Dijon mustard, beaten egg, Worcestershire sauce, lemon juice, Old Bay seasoning, salt, and pepper. Gently mix until well combined, being careful not to break up the crab meat too much. The mixture should hold together when shaped into patties.
2. Shape the crab cakes:
    - Divide the crab mixture into equal portions and shape them into round patties, about 1/2 to 3/4 inch thick. You should get about 6-8 crab cakes, depending on the size you prefer. Place the formed crab cakes on a baking sheet lined with parchment paper.
3. Coat the crab cakes:
    - Place the flour in a shallow dish. Lightly dredge each crab cake in the flour, shaking off any excess.

4. Cook the crab cakes:
   - In a large skillet, heat the butter and olive oil over medium heat until the butter is melted and the oil is hot but not smoking. Carefully place the crab cakes in the skillet, being careful not to overcrowd the pan. Cook the crab cakes in batches if necessary.
   - Cook the crab cakes for about 3-4 minutes on each side, or until they are golden brown and crispy. Use a spatula to carefully flip them halfway through cooking.
   - Once cooked, transfer the crab cakes to a paper towel-lined plate to drain any excess oil.
5. Serve:
   - Serve the Dungeness crab cakes hot, with lemon wedges on the side for squeezing. You can also serve them with tartar sauce or aioli for dipping, if desired.
   - Garnish with additional chopped parsley or green onions, if desired.

Enjoy your delicious homemade Dungeness Crab Cakes!

Hazelnut Crusted Salmon

Ingredients:

- 4 salmon fillets (about 6 ounces each), skin removed
- 1 cup hazelnuts, finely chopped or ground
- 1/2 cup breadcrumbs (preferably Panko)
- 2 tablespoons fresh parsley, finely chopped
- 2 tablespoons Dijon mustard
- 2 tablespoons honey
- 2 tablespoons olive oil
- Salt and pepper to taste
- Lemon wedges, for serving
- Fresh parsley, for garnish (optional)

Instructions:

1. Preheat the oven:
    - Preheat your oven to 400°F (200°C). Line a baking sheet with parchment paper or lightly grease it with olive oil to prevent sticking.
2. Prepare the hazelnut crust:
    - In a shallow dish, combine the finely chopped or ground hazelnuts with the breadcrumbs and chopped parsley. Season with a pinch of salt and pepper, and mix well to combine.
3. Coat the salmon:
    - In a separate bowl, whisk together the Dijon mustard and honey until well combined. Brush each salmon fillet generously with the mustard-honey mixture, coating both sides.
4. Apply the hazelnut crust:
    - Press each mustard-coated salmon fillet into the hazelnut mixture, coating the top side thoroughly. Gently pat the mixture onto the salmon to ensure it adheres well.
5. Cook the salmon:
    - Place the hazelnut-crusted salmon fillets on the prepared baking sheet, spacing them apart to allow for even cooking.
    - Drizzle a little olive oil over the top of each salmon fillet to help with browning.

- Bake the salmon in the preheated oven for 12-15 minutes, or until the fish is cooked through and the crust is golden brown and crispy. The internal temperature of the salmon should reach 145°F (63°C) when properly cooked.
6. Serve:
    - Once cooked, remove the hazelnut-crusted salmon from the oven and let it rest for a couple of minutes.
    - Serve the salmon hot, garnished with fresh parsley and lemon wedges on the side for squeezing.
    - You can serve the salmon with your favorite side dishes, such as roasted vegetables, steamed greens, or a fresh salad.

Enjoy your flavorful hazelnut-crusted salmon!

Tillamook Cheese Soup

Ingredients:

- 4 tablespoons unsalted butter
- 1 medium onion, diced
- 2 cloves garlic, minced
- 1/4 cup all-purpose flour
- 4 cups chicken or vegetable broth
- 2 cups whole milk
- 2 cups Tillamook Sharp Cheddar Cheese, grated
- 1 cup Tillamook Colby Jack Cheese, grated
- 1/2 cup Tillamook Pepper Jack Cheese, grated (for a spicy kick, optional)
- 1/2 cup heavy cream
- 1 teaspoon Dijon mustard
- Salt and pepper to taste
- Chopped chives or green onions for garnish (optional)

Instructions:

1. Saute onions and garlic:
    - In a large pot or Dutch oven, melt the butter over medium heat. Add the diced onion and minced garlic, and sauté until softened and translucent, about 5 minutes.
2. Make roux:
    - Sprinkle the flour over the onions and garlic, stirring constantly to cook the flour for about 2 minutes. This will help thicken the soup.
3. Add liquids:
    - Gradually pour in the chicken or vegetable broth and milk, stirring constantly to prevent lumps from forming. Bring the mixture to a gentle simmer, stirring occasionally.
4. Add cheese:
    - Once the soup is simmering, gradually add the grated Tillamook cheeses, stirring until they melt and the soup becomes smooth and creamy. Reserve a small amount of cheese for garnish if desired.
5. Finish the soup:
    - Stir in the heavy cream and Dijon mustard, then season with salt and pepper to taste. If you prefer a spicier soup, you can add some finely chopped jalapeños or a pinch of cayenne pepper at this stage.

6. Simmer and serve:
   - Allow the soup to simmer gently for another 5-10 minutes to allow the flavors to meld together. Stir occasionally to prevent the cheese from sticking to the bottom of the pot.
   - Once the soup is heated through and creamy, ladle it into bowls. Garnish with a sprinkle of grated Tillamook cheese and chopped chives or green onions if desired.
7. Enjoy:
   - Serve the Tillamook Cheese Soup hot, with crusty bread or crackers on the side for dipping. Enjoy the rich and comforting flavors of this delicious soup!

This Tillamook Cheese Soup is sure to be a hit with cheese lovers. Feel free to customize the recipe with your favorite Tillamook cheese varieties for a unique flavor profile.

Oregon Pinot Noir Braised Lamb Shanks

Ingredients:

- 4 lamb shanks, about 1 to 1.5 pounds each
- Salt and pepper to taste
- 2 tablespoons olive oil
- 1 large onion, chopped
- 2 carrots, chopped
- 2 celery stalks, chopped
- 4 garlic cloves, minced
- 2 cups Oregon Pinot Noir wine
- 2 cups beef or vegetable broth
- 2 tablespoons tomato paste
- 2 sprigs fresh rosemary
- 2 sprigs fresh thyme
- 2 bay leaves
- 1 tablespoon balsamic vinegar
- 1 tablespoon honey or brown sugar (optional, to balance acidity)
- Chopped fresh parsley for garnish

Instructions:

1. Preheat the oven: Preheat your oven to 325°F (160°C).
2. Season the lamb shanks: Season the lamb shanks generously with salt and pepper on all sides.
3. Sear the lamb shanks: Heat the olive oil in a large oven-safe Dutch oven or heavy-bottomed pot over medium-high heat. Once hot, add the lamb shanks and sear them until browned on all sides, about 3-4 minutes per side. Remove the lamb shanks from the pot and set them aside.
4. Saute the vegetables: In the same pot, add the chopped onion, carrots, and celery. Cook, stirring occasionally, until the vegetables are softened, about 5 minutes. Add the minced garlic and cook for an additional minute.
5. Deglaze the pot: Pour the Oregon Pinot Noir wine into the pot, scraping the bottom with a wooden spoon to loosen any browned bits (fond). Allow the wine to simmer for a few minutes to reduce slightly.
6. Braise the lamb shanks: Return the lamb shanks to the pot, nestling them among the vegetables. Add the beef or vegetable broth, tomato paste, rosemary, thyme, and bay leaves. Bring the liquid to a simmer.

7. Cover and braise in the oven: Cover the pot with a lid and transfer it to the preheated oven. Braise the lamb shanks in the oven for about 2.5 to 3 hours, or until the meat is fork-tender and falling off the bone.
8. Finish the sauce: Once the lamb shanks are done, remove them from the pot and set them aside. Skim any excess fat from the surface of the braising liquid. If the sauce is too thin, you can simmer it on the stovetop to reduce and thicken it. Stir in the balsamic vinegar and honey or brown sugar (if using) to balance the acidity and sweetness of the sauce.
9. Serve: Return the lamb shanks to the pot and coat them with the sauce. Serve the Oregon Pinot Noir Braised Lamb Shanks hot, garnished with chopped fresh parsley for a pop of color and freshness.
10. Enjoy: Serve the lamb shanks with your choice of side dishes, such as mashed potatoes, polenta, or roasted vegetables. The tender meat and flavorful sauce are sure to impress your guests!

This dish pairs beautifully with a glass of Oregon Pinot Noir wine, enhancing the rich flavors of the braised lamb shanks. Enjoy!

Oregon Hazelnut Pesto Pasta

Ingredients:

For the pesto:

- 1 cup Oregon hazelnuts, toasted and peeled
- 2 cups fresh basil leaves, packed
- 2 cloves garlic
- 1/2 cup grated Parmesan cheese
- 1/4 cup extra virgin olive oil
- Salt and pepper to taste

For the pasta:

- 12 ounces pasta of your choice (spaghetti, fettuccine, penne, etc.)
- Salt for boiling water
- Extra grated Parmesan cheese for serving
- Fresh basil leaves for garnish (optional)

Instructions:

1. Prepare the hazelnuts:
   - Preheat your oven to 350°F (175°C). Spread the hazelnuts in a single layer on a baking sheet and toast them in the oven for about 10-12 minutes, or until lightly browned and fragrant. Remove from the oven and let them cool slightly. Once cooled, rub the hazelnuts with a clean kitchen towel to remove the skins.
2. Cook the pasta:
   - Bring a large pot of salted water to a boil. Cook the pasta according to the package instructions until al dente. Reserve about 1/2 cup of the pasta cooking water before draining the pasta. Set the drained pasta aside.
3. Make the hazelnut pesto:
   - In a food processor, combine the toasted hazelnuts, fresh basil leaves, garlic cloves, and grated Parmesan cheese. Pulse until the ingredients are finely chopped and well combined.

- With the food processor running, slowly drizzle in the extra virgin olive oil until the pesto reaches your desired consistency. If it's too thick, you can add a little more olive oil. Season with salt and pepper to taste, and pulse to combine.
4. Combine the pesto and pasta:
    - In a large mixing bowl, toss the cooked pasta with the hazelnut pesto until evenly coated. If the pesto is too thick, you can add some of the reserved pasta cooking water to loosen it up and help it coat the pasta more easily.
5. Serve:
    - Divide the hazelnut pesto pasta among serving plates or bowls. Sprinkle extra grated Parmesan cheese on top and garnish with fresh basil leaves, if desired.
    - Serve the Oregon Hazelnut Pesto Pasta immediately, while it's still warm and the flavors are fresh.

This dish is perfect for a quick and delicious weeknight dinner or a special occasion.

The nutty flavor of the hazelnuts adds a unique twist to the classic pesto sauce, making it a memorable and satisfying meal. Enjoy!

Pacific Northwest Clam Chowder

Ingredients:

- 2 pounds fresh Pacific Northwest clams, scrubbed clean
- 4 slices bacon, chopped
- 1 tablespoon unsalted butter
- 1 large onion, finely diced
- 2 stalks celery, finely diced
- 2 medium carrots, finely diced
- 2 cloves garlic, minced
- 2 cups Yukon Gold potatoes, diced
- 4 cups clam juice or fish stock
- 1 cup heavy cream
- 1/2 cup whole milk
- 2 bay leaves
- 1 teaspoon fresh thyme leaves
- Salt and pepper to taste
- Chopped fresh parsley for garnish
- Oyster crackers or crusty bread for serving

Instructions:

1. Prepare the clams:
    - In a large pot, add 1 cup of water and bring it to a boil over medium-high heat. Add the cleaned clams to the pot, cover, and steam for about 5-7 minutes, or until the clams have opened.
    - Remove the pot from the heat and transfer the clams to a bowl, discarding any clams that did not open. Strain and reserve the clam cooking liquid for later use. Once the clams are cool enough to handle, remove the meat from the shells and roughly chop them. Set aside.
2. Cook the bacon and vegetables:
    - In a large Dutch oven or soup pot, cook the chopped bacon over medium heat until crisp. Remove the bacon with a slotted spoon and transfer it to a paper towel-lined plate to drain. Set aside.
    - In the same pot, add the butter and diced onion, celery, and carrots. Cook, stirring occasionally, until the vegetables are softened, about 5-7 minutes. Add the minced garlic and cook for an additional minute.

3. Add the potatoes and liquid:
    - Add the diced potatoes to the pot, along with the reserved clam cooking liquid and clam juice or fish stock. Bring the mixture to a simmer and cook until the potatoes are tender, about 10-12 minutes.
4. Make the chowder base:
    - Once the potatoes are cooked, stir in the heavy cream, whole milk, bay leaves, and fresh thyme leaves. Season the chowder with salt and pepper to taste. Let the chowder simmer gently for another 5 minutes to allow the flavors to meld together.
5. Finish the chowder:
    - Add the chopped clams and cooked bacon to the chowder, stirring to combine. Let the chowder simmer for an additional 2-3 minutes to heat through.
    - Taste the chowder and adjust the seasoning if needed.
6. Serve:
    - Ladle the Pacific Northwest Clam Chowder into bowls and garnish with chopped fresh parsley. Serve hot with oyster crackers or crusty bread on the side for dipping.

Enjoy this delicious and comforting Pacific Northwest Clam Chowder, perfect for a cozy meal on a chilly day!

Oregon Blackberry Cobbler

Ingredients:

For the filling:

- 6 cups fresh Oregon blackberries
- 1/2 cup granulated sugar
- 2 tablespoons cornstarch
- 1 tablespoon lemon juice
- 1 teaspoon vanilla extract

For the topping:

- 1 cup all-purpose flour
- 1/2 cup granulated sugar
- 1 teaspoon baking powder
- 1/4 teaspoon salt
- 1/2 cup unsalted butter, chilled and cut into small pieces
- 1/4 cup boiling water

Instructions:

1. Preheat your oven to 375°F (190°C). Grease a 9x13-inch baking dish or a similar-sized baking pan.
2. In a large bowl, gently toss together the blackberries, sugar, cornstarch, lemon juice, and vanilla extract until the blackberries are evenly coated. Pour the blackberry mixture into the prepared baking dish and spread it out evenly.
3. In another bowl, combine the flour, sugar, baking powder, and salt. Add the chilled butter pieces and use a pastry cutter or your fingers to cut the butter into the dry ingredients until the mixture resembles coarse crumbs.
4. Gradually add the boiling water to the flour mixture, stirring until a thick batter forms. Drop spoonfuls of the batter over the blackberry filling in the baking dish, covering it as evenly as possible.
5. Bake the cobbler in the preheated oven for 45 to 50 minutes, or until the topping is golden brown and the filling is bubbly around the edges.
6. Remove the cobbler from the oven and let it cool for a few minutes before serving. Serve warm, optionally with a scoop of vanilla ice cream or a dollop of whipped cream.
7. Enjoy your delicious Oregon Blackberry Cobbler!

Grilled Oregon Coast Oysters

Ingredients:

- Fresh Oregon Coast oysters (as many as desired)
- 1/2 cup butter, melted
- 2 cloves garlic, minced
- 1 tablespoon fresh parsley, chopped
- 1 tablespoon lemon juice
- Salt and pepper to taste
- Lemon wedges for serving

Instructions:

1. Preheat your grill to medium-high heat.
2. While the grill is heating up, prepare the garlic herb butter. In a small bowl, mix together the melted butter, minced garlic, chopped parsley, lemon juice, salt, and pepper. Set aside.
3. Scrub the oysters under cold running water to remove any dirt or debris. Use an oyster knife to shuck the oysters, discarding the top shell and loosening the oyster from the bottom shell.
4. Arrange the shucked oysters on a grill-safe tray or sheet pan.
5. Spoon a small amount of the garlic herb butter onto each oyster, distributing it evenly.
6. Carefully place the tray of oysters on the preheated grill. Close the lid and cook the oysters for about 5-7 minutes, or until the edges of the oysters start to curl and the butter is bubbling.
7. Using tongs or a heatproof glove, carefully remove the tray of grilled oysters from the grill.
8. Serve the grilled Oregon Coast oysters immediately, accompanied by lemon wedges for squeezing over the top.
9. Enjoy the succulent flavor of the ocean with each bite of these perfectly grilled oysters, a true taste of the Oregon Coast!

Whether enjoyed as an appetizer or a main course, grilled Oregon Coast oysters are sure to impress with their fresh, briny taste and savory garlic herb butter.

Huckleberry Pancakes

Ingredients:

- 1 cup all-purpose flour
- 2 tablespoons granulated sugar
- 1 teaspoon baking powder
- 1/2 teaspoon baking soda
- 1/4 teaspoon salt
- 1 egg
- 1 cup buttermilk
- 2 tablespoons unsalted butter, melted
- 1/2 cup fresh huckleberries (or thawed frozen huckleberries)
- Butter or oil for cooking
- Maple syrup for serving

Instructions:

1. In a large mixing bowl, whisk together the flour, sugar, baking powder, baking soda, and salt until well combined.
2. In a separate bowl, beat the egg, then add the buttermilk and melted butter. Stir until smooth.
3. Pour the wet ingredients into the dry ingredients and stir until just combined. Be careful not to overmix; a few lumps are okay. Fold in the huckleberries gently.
4. Heat a non-stick skillet or griddle over medium heat and lightly grease with butter or oil.
5. Pour about 1/4 cup of batter onto the skillet for each pancake, spreading it slightly with the back of a spoon to form a round shape.
6. Cook the pancakes for 2-3 minutes, or until bubbles start to form on the surface and the edges look set.
7. Carefully flip the pancakes using a spatula and cook for an additional 1-2 minutes on the other side, or until golden brown and cooked through.
8. Transfer the cooked pancakes to a plate and keep warm while you cook the remaining batter, adding more butter or oil to the skillet as needed.
9. Serve the huckleberry pancakes warm, drizzled with maple syrup.
10. Enjoy the delicious flavor of huckleberries in every fluffy bite of these homemade pancakes!

Whether enjoyed for breakfast or brunch, huckleberry pancakes are sure to become a favorite with their burst of fruity goodness and fluffy texture.

Wild Mushroom Risotto

Ingredients:

- 1 cup Arborio rice
- 4 cups chicken or vegetable broth
- 1/2 cup dry white wine
- 2 tablespoons olive oil
- 2 tablespoons unsalted butter
- 1 small onion, finely chopped
- 2 cloves garlic, minced
- 8 ounces mixed wild mushrooms (such as shiitake, cremini, and oyster), cleaned and sliced
- 1/2 cup grated Parmesan cheese
- Salt and pepper to taste
- Fresh parsley, chopped (for garnish)

Instructions:

1. In a saucepan, heat the chicken or vegetable broth over medium heat until simmering. Reduce the heat to low and keep the broth warm.
2. In a separate large saucepan or Dutch oven, heat the olive oil and 1 tablespoon of butter over medium heat. Add the chopped onion and cook until softened, about 3-4 minutes. Add the minced garlic and cook for an additional 1-2 minutes, until fragrant.
3. Add the Arborio rice to the saucepan and stir to coat it with the oil and butter. Cook for 1-2 minutes, stirring frequently, until the rice is lightly toasted.
4. Pour in the dry white wine and cook, stirring constantly, until the wine has been absorbed by the rice.
5. Begin adding the warm broth to the rice, one ladleful at a time, stirring constantly and allowing each addition of broth to be absorbed before adding more. Continue this process until the rice is creamy and cooked al dente, about 18-20 minutes.
6. While the risotto is cooking, heat the remaining tablespoon of butter in a skillet over medium heat. Add the sliced wild mushrooms and sauté until they are tender and golden brown, about 5-7 minutes. Season with salt and pepper to taste.
7. Once the risotto is cooked, stir in the sautéed mushrooms and grated Parmesan cheese. Taste and adjust seasoning with salt and pepper if needed.

8. Serve the wild mushroom risotto hot, garnished with chopped fresh parsley and additional grated Parmesan cheese if desired.
9. Enjoy the rich and creamy texture of this indulgent wild mushroom risotto, perfect for a cozy dinner or special occasion!

This dish pairs beautifully with a crisp green salad and a glass of your favorite white wine.

Marionberry BBQ Sauce

Ingredients:

- 1 cup fresh or frozen Marionberries (thawed if frozen)
- 1 cup ketchup
- 1/4 cup apple cider vinegar
- 1/4 cup brown sugar
- 2 tablespoons Worcestershire sauce
- 2 cloves garlic, minced
- 1 teaspoon smoked paprika
- 1/2 teaspoon onion powder
- 1/2 teaspoon ground mustard
- Salt and pepper to taste

Instructions:

1. In a saucepan, combine the Marionberries, ketchup, apple cider vinegar, brown sugar, Worcestershire sauce, minced garlic, smoked paprika, onion powder, and ground mustard.
2. Place the saucepan over medium heat and bring the mixture to a simmer, stirring occasionally.
3. Once the mixture is simmering, reduce the heat to low and let it cook for about 15-20 minutes, stirring occasionally, until the Marionberries have softened and the sauce has thickened.
4. Remove the saucepan from the heat and let the sauce cool slightly.
5. Once the sauce has cooled a bit, use an immersion blender or transfer the mixture to a blender or food processor to puree until smooth. Alternatively, you can leave the sauce slightly chunky if you prefer.
6. Taste the BBQ sauce and adjust the seasoning with salt and pepper as needed.
7. Transfer the Marionberry BBQ Sauce to a jar or airtight container and store it in the refrigerator until ready to use.
8. Use the Marionberry BBQ Sauce as a delicious glaze for grilled chicken, pork ribs, or tofu. Brush it on during the last few minutes of grilling for a sweet and tangy finish.
9. Enjoy the unique flavor of Marionberries in this homemade BBQ sauce, perfect for adding a taste of Oregon to your favorite barbecue dishes!

This Marionberry BBQ Sauce can also be used as a dipping sauce for appetizers like chicken wings or as a flavorful condiment for burgers and sandwiches.

Oregon Trail Mix

Ingredients:

- 1 cup raw almonds
- 1 cup raw hazelnuts (also known as filberts)
- 1 cup dried cranberries
- 1 cup dried blueberries
- 1 cup roasted pumpkin seeds (pepitas)
- 1 cup dark chocolate chips or chunks
- 1 cup coconut flakes (unsweetened)
- Optional: 1 teaspoon sea salt

Instructions:

1. Preheat your oven to 350°F (175°C). Line a baking sheet with parchment paper or a silicone baking mat.
2. Spread the almonds and hazelnuts in a single layer on the prepared baking sheet. Roast in the preheated oven for 8-10 minutes, or until fragrant and lightly golden. Keep an eye on them to prevent burning.
3. Remove the baking sheet from the oven and let the nuts cool completely.
4. In a large mixing bowl, combine the cooled almonds and hazelnuts with the dried cranberries, dried blueberries, roasted pumpkin seeds, dark chocolate chips or chunks, and coconut flakes. If desired, sprinkle with sea salt for a sweet and salty flavor contrast.
5. Toss the ingredients together until evenly distributed.
6. Transfer the Oregon Trail Mix to an airtight container or portion it into individual snack bags for convenient grab-and-go snacking.
7. Enjoy this wholesome and flavorful trail mix as a nutritious snack while hiking, camping, or exploring the great outdoors, or simply as a tasty treat any time of day.

This Oregon-inspired trail mix is versatile and can be customized to suit your taste preferences. Feel free to adjust the ingredients or add other favorite nuts, seeds, or dried fruits to make it your own.

Rogue River Blue Cheese Salad

Ingredients:

For the salad:

- Mixed salad greens (such as baby spinach, arugula, and butter lettuce)
- Cherry tomatoes, halved
- Sliced cucumber
- Sliced red onion
- Toasted walnuts or pecans
- Crumbled Rogue River Blue Cheese

For the vinaigrette:

- 1/4 cup extra virgin olive oil
- 2 tablespoons balsamic vinegar
- 1 teaspoon Dijon mustard
- 1 teaspoon honey
- Salt and pepper to taste

Instructions:

1. In a large salad bowl, combine the mixed salad greens, cherry tomatoes, sliced cucumber, sliced red onion, and toasted walnuts or pecans.
2. In a small bowl or jar, whisk together the extra virgin olive oil, balsamic vinegar, Dijon mustard, honey, salt, and pepper until well combined to make the vinaigrette.
3. Drizzle the vinaigrette over the salad ingredients in the bowl.
4. Gently toss the salad until the ingredients are evenly coated with the vinaigrette.
5. Sprinkle crumbled Rogue River Blue Cheese over the top of the salad.
6. Serve the Rogue River Blue Cheese Salad immediately as a flavorful and elegant starter or side dish.
7. Enjoy the combination of fresh, vibrant flavors and creamy, tangy cheese in this delightful salad inspired by the flavors of Oregon.

This salad is versatile and can be customized with additional ingredients such as fresh berries, avocado slices, or grilled chicken for added flavor and protein. It pairs beautifully with a glass of Oregon Pinot Noir or a crisp white wine.

Hazelnut Crusted Chicken

Ingredients:

- 4 boneless, skinless chicken breasts
- 1 cup hazelnuts, finely chopped
- 1/2 cup breadcrumbs
- 1/4 cup grated Parmesan cheese
- 1 teaspoon dried thyme
- 1 teaspoon dried rosemary
- 1/2 teaspoon garlic powder
- Salt and pepper to taste
- 2 eggs
- 2 tablespoons olive oil
- Lemon wedges for serving (optional)

Instructions:

1. Preheat your oven to 375°F (190°C). Line a baking sheet with parchment paper or lightly grease it with cooking spray.
2. In a shallow dish, combine the finely chopped hazelnuts, breadcrumbs, grated Parmesan cheese, dried thyme, dried rosemary, garlic powder, salt, and pepper. Mix well to combine.
3. In another shallow dish, beat the eggs until well mixed.
4. Season the chicken breasts with salt and pepper on both sides.
5. Dip each chicken breast into the beaten eggs, coating both sides.
6. Press the egg-coated chicken breasts into the hazelnut mixture, ensuring that the chicken is evenly coated with the nut mixture on both sides. Press the coating gently onto the chicken to help it adhere.
7. Place the coated chicken breasts onto the prepared baking sheet.
8. Drizzle olive oil evenly over the tops of the coated chicken breasts.
9. Bake the hazelnut crusted chicken in the preheated oven for 20-25 minutes, or until the chicken is cooked through and the coating is golden brown and crispy.
10. Remove the chicken from the oven and let it rest for a few minutes before serving.
11. Serve the hazelnut crusted chicken hot, optionally with lemon wedges on the side for squeezing over the top.

12. Enjoy the delicious combination of tender chicken and crunchy hazelnuts in this flavorful and satisfying dish!

This hazelnut crusted chicken pairs well with a variety of side dishes, such as roasted vegetables, mashed potatoes, or a crisp green salad. It's perfect for a weeknight dinner or a special occasion meal.

Tillamook Ice Cream Sundae

Ingredients:

- Tillamook ice cream (flavors of your choice)
- Chocolate syrup
- Caramel sauce
- Chopped nuts (such as almonds, pecans, or walnuts)
- Whipped cream
- Maraschino cherries
- Optional: sprinkles, chocolate chips, cookie crumbles, or any other favorite toppings

Instructions:

1. Scoop your favorite flavors of Tillamook ice cream into a serving bowl or dish. You can choose one flavor or create a combination of flavors for added variety.
2. Drizzle chocolate syrup and caramel sauce generously over the scoops of ice cream.
3. Sprinkle chopped nuts over the top of the ice cream and sauces. This adds a satisfying crunch and nutty flavor to your sundae.
4. Add a dollop of whipped cream on top of the ice cream, creating a fluffy cloud-like layer.
5. Garnish your Tillamook Ice Cream Sundae with maraschino cherries for a pop of color and sweetness.
6. If desired, sprinkle additional toppings such as sprinkles, chocolate chips, or cookie crumbles over the whipped cream for added texture and flavor.
7. Serve your Tillamook Ice Cream Sundae immediately and enjoy the irresistible combination of creamy ice cream, decadent sauces, crunchy nuts, and sweet toppings.
8. Feel free to customize your sundae with your favorite flavors and toppings to create a dessert masterpiece that satisfies your sweet cravings.

Whether enjoyed as a special treat on a hot summer day or as a comforting dessert any time of year, a Tillamook Ice Cream Sundae is sure to delight your taste buds and bring a smile to your face.

Oregon Hazelnut Encrusted Halibut

Ingredients:

- 4 halibut fillets, skin removed
- 1 cup Oregon hazelnuts, finely chopped
- 1/2 cup breadcrumbs
- 1/4 cup grated Parmesan cheese
- 2 tablespoons fresh parsley, finely chopped
- 1 teaspoon dried thyme
- 1 teaspoon lemon zest
- Salt and pepper to taste
- 2 eggs, beaten
- 2 tablespoons olive oil
- Lemon wedges for serving

Instructions:

1. Preheat your oven to 400°F (200°C). Line a baking sheet with parchment paper or lightly grease it with olive oil.
2. In a shallow dish, combine the finely chopped Oregon hazelnuts, breadcrumbs, grated Parmesan cheese, fresh parsley, dried thyme, lemon zest, salt, and pepper. Mix well to combine.
3. Dip each halibut fillet into the beaten eggs, coating both sides evenly.
4. Press the egg-coated halibut fillets into the hazelnut mixture, ensuring that the fish is evenly coated with the nut mixture on all sides. Press the coating gently onto the fish to help it adhere.
5. Place the coated halibut fillets onto the prepared baking sheet.
6. Drizzle olive oil over the top of each halibut fillet to help the coating crisp up in the oven.
7. Bake the hazelnut-encrusted halibut in the preheated oven for about 15-20 minutes, or until the fish is cooked through and the coating is golden brown and crispy.
8. Once done, remove the halibut from the oven and let it rest for a couple of minutes before serving.
9. Serve the Oregon Hazelnut Encrusted Halibut hot, accompanied by lemon wedges for squeezing over the top.

10. Enjoy the exquisite combination of tender halibut with the crunchy texture and nutty flavor of the hazelnut crust, a perfect representation of Oregon's culinary heritage!

This dish pairs wonderfully with a side of roasted vegetables or a fresh salad dressed with a light vinaigrette. It's a fantastic choice for a special dinner occasion or anytime you want to savor the flavors of the Pacific Northwest.

Marionberry Jam

Ingredients:

- 4 cups fresh Marionberries
- 2 cups granulated sugar
- 2 tablespoons freshly squeezed lemon juice
- 1 tablespoon lemon zest
- 1 teaspoon pure vanilla extract (optional)

Instructions:

1. Rinse the Marionberries under cold water and drain them well. Remove any stems or leaves.
2. In a large, heavy-bottomed pot, combine the Marionberries, granulated sugar, freshly squeezed lemon juice, and lemon zest.
3. Place the pot over medium heat and stir the mixture continuously until the sugar has dissolved and the berries begin to release their juices. This usually takes about 5-7 minutes.
4. Once the sugar has dissolved and the berries have softened, you can use a potato masher or the back of a spoon to gently crush some of the berries, if desired, to release more juices and create a thicker jam.
5. Continue to cook the jam over medium heat, stirring frequently, until it thickens and reaches the desired consistency. This can take anywhere from 15 to 25 minutes, depending on how thick you want your jam to be.
6. To test if the jam is ready, you can use the "plate test" method: place a small spoonful of jam on a chilled plate and let it cool for a minute. Run your finger through the jam on the plate – if it wrinkles and holds its shape, it's ready. If it's still too runny, continue cooking the jam for a few more minutes and test again.
7. Once the jam has reached the desired consistency, remove the pot from the heat. If using vanilla extract, stir it into the jam at this point.
8. Ladle the hot Marionberry Jam into clean, sterilized jars, leaving about 1/4 inch of headspace at the top of each jar. Wipe the rims of the jars with a clean, damp cloth to remove any drips or spills.
9. Place the lids on the jars and screw on the bands until they are fingertip tight.
10. Process the filled jars in a boiling water bath for 10 minutes to ensure proper sealing and preservation. If you're not processing the jars, let them cool

completely before storing them in the refrigerator. The jam will keep in the refrigerator for up to 3 weeks.
11. Once opened, store the Marionberry Jam in the refrigerator and enjoy it spread on toast, muffins, scones, or as a topping for yogurt or ice cream.
12. Enjoy the sweet, fruity flavor of homemade Marionberry Jam, capturing the essence of Oregon's bountiful berry harvest!

Oregon Pear Salad with Blue Cheese

Ingredients:

For the salad:

- 4 cups mixed salad greens (such as baby spinach, arugula, and butter lettuce)
- 2 ripe Oregon pears, thinly sliced
- 1/2 cup crumbled blue cheese (such as Rogue River Blue Cheese)
- 1/4 cup toasted walnuts or pecans, chopped
- Optional: dried cranberries or pomegranate arils for extra sweetness and color

For the vinaigrette:

- 1/4 cup extra virgin olive oil
- 2 tablespoons balsamic vinegar
- 1 teaspoon Dijon mustard
- 1 teaspoon honey
- Salt and pepper to taste

Instructions:

1. In a large salad bowl, combine the mixed salad greens, thinly sliced Oregon pears, crumbled blue cheese, and toasted walnuts or pecans. If using, add dried cranberries or pomegranate arils for additional sweetness and color.
2. In a small bowl or jar, whisk together the extra virgin olive oil, balsamic vinegar, Dijon mustard, honey, salt, and pepper to make the vinaigrette.
3. Drizzle the vinaigrette over the salad ingredients in the bowl.
4. Gently toss the salad until the ingredients are evenly coated with the vinaigrette.
5. Serve the Oregon Pear Salad with Blue Cheese immediately as a flavorful and elegant starter or side dish.
6. Enjoy the delicious combination of sweet, juicy pears, creamy blue cheese, and crunchy nuts, all brought together by the tangy vinaigrette dressing, a perfect representation of Oregon's fresh and vibrant flavors!

This salad is versatile and can be customized with additional ingredients such as avocado slices, crispy bacon, or grilled chicken for added flavor and protein. It's perfect for a light lunch, a refreshing side dish, or as part of a festive meal.

Grilled Columbia River Steelhead

Ingredients:

For the salad:

- 4 cups mixed salad greens (such as baby spinach, arugula, and butter lettuce)
- 2 ripe Oregon pears, thinly sliced
- 1/2 cup crumbled blue cheese (such as Rogue River Blue Cheese)
- 1/4 cup toasted walnuts or pecans, chopped
- Optional: dried cranberries or pomegranate arils for extra sweetness and color

For the vinaigrette:

- 1/4 cup extra virgin olive oil
- 2 tablespoons balsamic vinegar
- 1 teaspoon Dijon mustard
- 1 teaspoon honey
- Salt and pepper to taste

Instructions:

1. In a large salad bowl, combine the mixed salad greens, thinly sliced Oregon pears, crumbled blue cheese, and toasted walnuts or pecans. If using, add dried cranberries or pomegranate arils for additional sweetness and color.
2. In a small bowl or jar, whisk together the extra virgin olive oil, balsamic vinegar, Dijon mustard, honey, salt, and pepper to make the vinaigrette.
3. Drizzle the vinaigrette over the salad ingredients in the bowl.
4. Gently toss the salad until the ingredients are evenly coated with the vinaigrette.
5. Serve the Oregon Pear Salad with Blue Cheese immediately as a flavorful and elegant starter or side dish.
6. Enjoy the delicious combination of sweet, juicy pears, creamy blue cheese, and crunchy nuts, all brought together by the tangy vinaigrette dressing, a perfect representation of Oregon's fresh and vibrant flavors!

This salad is versatile and can be customized with additional ingredients such as avocado slices, crispy bacon, or grilled chicken for added flavor and protein. It's perfect for a light lunch, a refreshing side dish, or as part of a festive meal.

Hazelnut Butter Cookies

Ingredients:

- 1 cup unsalted butter, softened
- 1 cup hazelnut butter
- 1 cup granulated sugar
- 1 cup packed brown sugar
- 2 eggs
- 1 teaspoon vanilla extract
- 2 1/2 cups all-purpose flour
- 1 teaspoon baking powder
- 1 teaspoon baking soda
- 1/2 teaspoon salt
- Additional granulated sugar for rolling (optional)
- Whole hazelnuts for decoration (optional)

Instructions:

1. Preheat your oven to 350°F (175°C). Line baking sheets with parchment paper or silicone baking mats.
2. In a large mixing bowl, cream together the softened butter, hazelnut butter, granulated sugar, and brown sugar until light and fluffy.
3. Beat in the eggs, one at a time, until well combined. Stir in the vanilla extract.
4. In a separate bowl, whisk together the all-purpose flour, baking powder, baking soda, and salt.
5. Gradually add the dry ingredients to the wet ingredients, mixing until a smooth dough forms.
6. If desired, shape the dough into small balls, about 1 inch in diameter. Roll each ball in granulated sugar for added sweetness and texture.
7. Place the cookie dough balls onto the prepared baking sheets, spacing them about 2 inches apart. If using, gently press a whole hazelnut into the center of each cookie for decoration.
8. Bake the cookies in the preheated oven for 10-12 minutes, or until the edges are golden brown.
9. Remove the cookies from the oven and let them cool on the baking sheets for a few minutes before transferring them to wire racks to cool completely.
10. Once cooled, serve and enjoy these delicious Hazelnut Butter Cookies with a glass of milk or your favorite hot beverage.

11. Store any leftovers in an airtight container at room temperature for up to one week.

These Hazelnut Butter Cookies are perfect for enjoying as a snack, dessert, or for sharing with friends and family during special occasions. Their nutty flavor and buttery texture make them irresistible to cookie lovers of all ages.

Tillamook Cheesecake

Ingredients:

For the crust:

- 1 1/2 cups graham cracker crumbs
- 1/4 cup granulated sugar
- 1/2 cup unsalted butter, melted

For the cheesecake filling:

- 24 ounces (three 8-ounce packages) cream cheese, softened
- 1 cup granulated sugar
- 1 teaspoon vanilla extract
- 3 large eggs
- 1 cup sour cream
- 1/4 cup all-purpose flour
- 1/2 cup Tillamook cheddar cheese, shredded

For the topping:

- 1 cup sour cream
- 2 tablespoons granulated sugar
- 1 teaspoon vanilla extract

Instructions:

1. Preheat your oven to 325°F (160°C). Grease a 9-inch springform pan and wrap the outside with aluminum foil to prevent any leakage.
2. In a mixing bowl, combine the graham cracker crumbs, granulated sugar, and melted butter until the mixture resembles coarse sand.
3. Press the crumb mixture into the bottom of the prepared springform pan, using the back of a spoon or your fingers to pack it down firmly.
4. In a large mixing bowl, beat the softened cream cheese, granulated sugar, and vanilla extract until smooth and creamy.
5. Add the eggs one at a time, beating well after each addition.
6. Stir in the sour cream and flour until well combined.
7. Gently fold in the shredded Tillamook cheddar cheese until evenly distributed throughout the batter.

8. Pour the cheesecake filling over the prepared crust in the springform pan, spreading it out evenly with a spatula.
9. Place the springform pan in a larger roasting pan or baking dish. Fill the larger pan with hot water until it reaches halfway up the sides of the springform pan. This water bath helps prevent cracks in the cheesecake.
10. Bake the cheesecake in the preheated oven for 50-60 minutes, or until the edges are set but the center is still slightly jiggly.
11. While the cheesecake is baking, prepare the topping by mixing together the sour cream, granulated sugar, and vanilla extract until smooth.
12. After the cheesecake has finished baking, remove it from the oven and carefully spread the sour cream topping over the surface.
13. Return the cheesecake to the oven and bake for an additional 5 minutes.
14. Turn off the oven and leave the cheesecake inside with the door slightly ajar for about 1 hour to cool gradually.
15. Once cooled, refrigerate the cheesecake for at least 4 hours, or preferably overnight, to set completely.
16. Before serving, carefully remove the sides of the springform pan and transfer the cheesecake to a serving platter.
17. Slice and serve your delicious Tillamook Cheesecake, garnished with fresh berries or a drizzle of caramel sauce if desired.
18. Enjoy the creamy texture and rich flavor of this indulgent cheesecake, showcasing the exceptional quality of Tillamook cheese!

Oregon Coast Seafood Linguine

Ingredients:

- 12 ounces linguine pasta
- 1 pound mixed seafood (such as shrimp, scallops, and crabmeat), cleaned and deveined
- 2 tablespoons olive oil
- 4 cloves garlic, minced
- 1 small onion, finely chopped
- 1 bell pepper, diced
- 1 cup cherry tomatoes, halved
- 1/2 cup white wine (optional)
- 1 cup seafood broth or clam juice
- 1/2 cup heavy cream
- 1/4 cup grated Parmesan cheese
- 2 tablespoons fresh parsley, chopped
- Salt and pepper to taste
- Red pepper flakes (optional, for added heat)
- Lemon wedges for serving

Instructions:

1. Cook the linguine pasta according to the package instructions until al dente. Drain and set aside, reserving about 1/2 cup of pasta cooking water.
2. In a large skillet or pan, heat the olive oil over medium heat. Add the minced garlic and chopped onion, and sauté until softened and fragrant, about 2-3 minutes.
3. Add the diced bell pepper to the skillet and cook for an additional 2-3 minutes until slightly softened.
4. Stir in the mixed seafood (such as shrimp, scallops, and crabmeat) and cook until just opaque and cooked through, about 4-5 minutes.
5. Add the halved cherry tomatoes to the skillet and cook for another 2-3 minutes until they begin to soften.
6. If using, pour in the white wine and seafood broth or clam juice, and bring the mixture to a simmer. Allow it to simmer for 5-7 minutes to reduce slightly.
7. Stir in the heavy cream and grated Parmesan cheese, and season with salt, pepper, and red pepper flakes (if using) to taste.

8. Add the cooked linguine pasta to the skillet, along with the chopped fresh parsley. Toss everything together until the pasta is well coated in the seafood sauce. If the sauce is too thick, you can add some of the reserved pasta cooking water to loosen it up.
9. Remove the skillet from the heat and serve the Oregon Coast Seafood Linguine immediately, garnished with additional chopped parsley and lemon wedges on the side.
10. Enjoy this flavorful and satisfying pasta dish, inspired by the bounty of the Oregon coast!

This Oregon Coast Seafood Linguine is perfect for a special dinner occasion or whenever you're craving a taste of the sea. Serve it with a crisp green salad and a glass of your favorite white wine for a complete meal.

Marionberry Muffins

Ingredients:

- 1 3/4 cups all-purpose flour
- 1/2 cup granulated sugar
- 2 teaspoons baking powder
- 1/2 teaspoon baking soda
- 1/4 teaspoon salt
- 1/2 cup unsalted butter, melted and cooled
- 2 large eggs
- 1 teaspoon vanilla extract
- 3/4 cup buttermilk
- 1 1/2 cups fresh or frozen Marionberries
- Turbinado sugar (optional, for sprinkling on top)

Instructions:

1. Preheat your oven to 375°F (190°C). Line a muffin tin with paper liners or grease the muffin cups with butter or cooking spray.
2. In a large mixing bowl, whisk together the all-purpose flour, granulated sugar, baking powder, baking soda, and salt until well combined.
3. In a separate bowl, whisk together the melted butter, eggs, vanilla extract, and buttermilk until smooth.
4. Pour the wet ingredients into the dry ingredients and gently fold together using a spatula or wooden spoon. Be careful not to overmix; a few lumps in the batter are okay.
5. Gently fold in the Marionberries until evenly distributed throughout the batter.
6. Divide the batter evenly among the prepared muffin cups, filling each about two-thirds full.
7. If desired, sprinkle the tops of the muffins with a little turbinado sugar for added sweetness and texture.
8. Bake the Marionberry muffins in the preheated oven for 18-20 minutes, or until the tops are golden brown and a toothpick inserted into the center of a muffin comes out clean.
9. Remove the muffins from the oven and let them cool in the muffin tin for a few minutes before transferring them to a wire rack to cool completely.

10. Once cooled, serve the Marionberry muffins and enjoy them as a delicious breakfast treat or snack.
11. Store any leftover muffins in an airtight container at room temperature for up to 3 days, or freeze them for longer storage.
12. Enjoy the sweet and juicy flavor of Marionberries in these homemade muffins, perfect for enjoying any time of day!

These Marionberry muffins are moist, tender, and bursting with berry goodness, making them a favorite among berry lovers of all ages.

Hazelnut Crusted Pork Chops

Ingredients:

- 4 boneless pork chops
- 1 cup Oregon hazelnuts, finely chopped
- 1/2 cup breadcrumbs
- 1/4 cup grated Parmesan cheese
- 2 tablespoons fresh parsley, chopped
- 1 teaspoon dried thyme
- 1 teaspoon lemon zest
- Salt and pepper to taste
- 2 eggs
- 2 tablespoons olive oil

Instructions:

1. Preheat your oven to 375°F (190°C). Line a baking sheet with parchment paper or lightly grease it with cooking spray.
2. Season the pork chops with salt and pepper on both sides.
3. In a shallow dish, combine the finely chopped Oregon hazelnuts, breadcrumbs, grated Parmesan cheese, chopped fresh parsley, dried thyme, and lemon zest. Mix well to combine.
4. In another shallow dish, beat the eggs until well mixed.
5. Dip each pork chop into the beaten eggs, coating both sides evenly.
6. Press the egg-coated pork chops into the hazelnut mixture, ensuring that the meat is evenly coated with the nut mixture on both sides. Press the coating gently onto the pork chops to help it adhere.
7. Place the coated pork chops onto the prepared baking sheet.
8. Drizzle olive oil evenly over the tops of the coated pork chops.
9. Bake the hazelnut crusted pork chops in the preheated oven for 20-25 minutes, or until the pork is cooked through and the coating is golden brown and crispy.
10. Remove the pork chops from the oven and let them rest for a few minutes before serving.
11. Serve the hazelnut crusted pork chops hot, accompanied by your favorite side dishes, such as roasted vegetables or mashed potatoes.
12. Enjoy the delicious combination of tender pork chops and crunchy hazelnut coating in this flavorful and satisfying dish!

These Hazelnut Crusted Pork Chops are sure to become a family favorite, perfect for a weeknight dinner or special occasion meal. The nutty flavor of the hazelnuts adds a unique twist to classic pork chops, creating a dish that's both comforting and elegant.

Tillamook Macaroni and Cheese

Ingredients:

- 8 ounces elbow macaroni or your favorite pasta shape
- 4 tablespoons unsalted butter
- 1/4 cup all-purpose flour
- 2 cups whole milk
- 2 cups Tillamook sharp cheddar cheese, shredded
- 1 cup Tillamook medium cheddar cheese, shredded
- 1/2 teaspoon salt, or to taste
- 1/4 teaspoon black pepper, or to taste
- Optional toppings: breadcrumbs, additional shredded cheese, chopped fresh herbs

Instructions:

1. Cook the elbow macaroni according to the package instructions until al dente. Drain and set aside.
2. In a large saucepan or pot, melt the butter over medium heat.
3. Once the butter is melted, whisk in the all-purpose flour to form a roux. Cook the roux for 1-2 minutes, stirring constantly, until it becomes golden brown and fragrant.
4. Gradually pour in the whole milk while whisking continuously to prevent lumps from forming. Cook the mixture, stirring constantly, until it thickens and comes to a gentle boil, about 5-7 minutes.
5. Reduce the heat to low and stir in the shredded Tillamook sharp cheddar cheese and Tillamook medium cheddar cheese until melted and smooth. Season with salt and black pepper to taste.
6. Add the cooked macaroni to the cheese sauce and stir until well combined, ensuring that all the pasta is evenly coated with the cheesy sauce.
7. Preheat your oven broiler to high.
8. Transfer the macaroni and cheese mixture to a baking dish or oven-safe skillet.
9. If desired, sprinkle the top of the macaroni and cheese with breadcrumbs and additional shredded cheese for a crunchy topping.
10. Place the baking dish or skillet under the preheated broiler and broil for 2-3 minutes, or until the top is golden brown and bubbly.

11. Remove the macaroni and cheese from the oven and let it cool for a few minutes before serving.
12. Garnish with chopped fresh herbs, if desired, and serve the Tillamook Macaroni and Cheese hot as a comforting and satisfying meal.

This Tillamook Macaroni and Cheese recipe is sure to please cheese lovers of all ages with its rich, creamy texture and deliciously cheesy flavor. Enjoy it as a side dish or main course, and savor every cheesy bite!

Oregon Berry Smoothie

Ingredients:

- 1 cup mixed Oregon berries (such as strawberries, raspberries, blueberries, blackberries)
- 1 ripe banana, peeled and sliced
- 1/2 cup plain Greek yogurt
- 1/2 cup almond milk (or any milk of your choice)
- 1 tablespoon honey or maple syrup (optional, for added sweetness)
- Ice cubes (optional, for a chilled smoothie)

Instructions:

1. Rinse the mixed Oregon berries under cold water and drain them well. Remove any stems or leaves.
2. Place the mixed berries, sliced banana, plain Greek yogurt, almond milk, and honey or maple syrup (if using) in a blender.
3. If you prefer a colder smoothie, add a handful of ice cubes to the blender as well.
4. Blend all the ingredients together on high speed until smooth and creamy. If the smoothie is too thick, you can add more almond milk or water to reach your desired consistency.
5. Once the smoothie is well blended and smooth, taste and adjust the sweetness if necessary by adding more honey or maple syrup.
6. Pour the Oregon Berry Smoothie into glasses and serve immediately.
7. Garnish with additional fresh berries or mint leaves for an extra touch of freshness, if desired.
8. Enjoy this delicious and nutritious Oregon Berry Smoothie as a refreshing breakfast, snack, or post-workout drink.

This smoothie is packed with vitamins, antioxidants, and fiber from the mixed berries, while the banana and Greek yogurt add creaminess and a boost of protein. It's a fantastic way to start your day or refuel your energy levels with the natural goodness of Oregon berries.

Columbia River Salmon Salad

Ingredients:

For the salmon:

- 1 lb Columbia River salmon fillets
- Olive oil
- Salt and pepper to taste
- Lemon wedges for serving

For the salad:

- Mixed salad greens (such as spinach, arugula, and romaine lettuce)
- Cherry tomatoes, halved
- Cucumber, sliced
- Red onion, thinly sliced
- Avocado, sliced
- Crumbled feta cheese
- Kalamata olives, pitted
- Optional: sliced bell peppers, sliced radishes, roasted corn kernels

For the dressing:

- 1/4 cup extra virgin olive oil
- 2 tablespoons balsamic vinegar
- 1 teaspoon Dijon mustard
- 1 teaspoon honey
- Salt and pepper to taste

Instructions:

1. Preheat your grill to medium-high heat. Brush the salmon fillets with olive oil and season them generously with salt and pepper.
2. Grill the salmon fillets for 4-5 minutes per side, or until they are cooked through and flake easily with a fork. Cooking time may vary depending on the thickness of

the fillets. Squeeze fresh lemon juice over the cooked salmon and set aside to cool slightly.
3. While the salmon is grilling, prepare the salad ingredients. In a large salad bowl, combine the mixed salad greens, cherry tomatoes, cucumber, red onion, avocado, crumbled feta cheese, and Kalamata olives. Add any additional salad ingredients of your choice, such as sliced bell peppers, sliced radishes, or roasted corn kernels.
4. In a small bowl or jar, whisk together the extra virgin olive oil, balsamic vinegar, Dijon mustard, honey, salt, and pepper to make the dressing.
5. Once the salmon has cooled slightly, flake it into bite-sized pieces using a fork.
6. Add the flaked salmon to the salad bowl and toss everything together gently to combine.
7. Drizzle the dressing over the salad and toss again until everything is evenly coated with the dressing.
8. Serve the Columbia River Salmon Salad immediately, garnished with additional lemon wedges if desired.
9. Enjoy this delicious and nutritious salad as a light and satisfying meal, perfect for lunch or dinner.

This Columbia River Salmon Salad is not only flavorful and satisfying but also packed with omega-3 fatty acids, protein, and essential nutrients from the salmon and fresh vegetables. It's a fantastic way to enjoy the bounty of the Pacific Northwest and celebrate the flavors of the Columbia River region.

Hazelnut Toffee

Ingredients:

- 1 cup unsalted butter
- 1 cup granulated sugar
- 1/4 cup water
- 1 tablespoon light corn syrup
- 1 cup toasted hazelnuts, chopped
- 8 ounces semisweet or dark chocolate, chopped (optional)
- Sea salt flakes for garnish (optional)

Instructions:

1. Prepare a baking sheet by lining it with parchment paper or a silicone baking mat. Set aside.
2. In a heavy-bottomed saucepan, combine the unsalted butter, granulated sugar, water, and light corn syrup over medium heat.
3. Stir the mixture constantly until the butter is melted and the sugar has dissolved.
4. Once the mixture comes to a boil, insert a candy thermometer into the saucepan and continue to cook the mixture, without stirring, until it reaches 300°F (hard crack stage).
5. Carefully stir in the chopped toasted hazelnuts, ensuring that they are evenly distributed throughout the toffee mixture.
6. Immediately pour the hot toffee mixture onto the prepared baking sheet, spreading it out evenly with a spatula.
7. If desired, sprinkle the chopped chocolate over the hot toffee and let it sit for a minute or two to soften. Use an offset spatula or the back of a spoon to spread the melted chocolate evenly over the toffee.
8. If using, sprinkle sea salt flakes over the melted chocolate for a delicious contrast of flavors.
9. Allow the hazelnut toffee to cool completely at room temperature until the chocolate has set and the toffee has hardened.
10. Once cooled and set, break the toffee into bite-sized pieces using your hands or a knife.
11. Store the hazelnut toffee in an airtight container at room temperature for up to two weeks, or in the refrigerator for longer shelf life.

12. Enjoy this homemade hazelnut toffee as a delightful treat or package it up in decorative bags or boxes to give as gifts to friends and family.

Hazelnut toffee makes a wonderful homemade gift for special occasions or holidays, and it's also a delicious indulgence to enjoy anytime you're craving something sweet and satisfying.

Tillamook Cheeseburger

Ingredients:

For the burger patties:

- 1 lb ground beef (preferably 80% lean)
- Salt and pepper to taste
- 4 slices Tillamook cheddar cheese

For assembling the burgers:

- 4 hamburger buns
- Lettuce leaves
- Sliced tomatoes
- Sliced red onions
- Pickles
- Ketchup and mustard (optional)
- Mayonnaise (optional)

Instructions:

1. Preheat your grill or skillet over medium-high heat.
2. Divide the ground beef into four equal portions and shape each portion into a patty. Make an indentation in the center of each patty with your thumb to prevent it from puffing up while cooking. Season both sides of the patties with salt and pepper.
3. Place the burger patties on the preheated grill or skillet and cook for 4-5 minutes on each side, or until they reach your desired level of doneness. During the last minute of cooking, place a slice of Tillamook cheddar cheese on top of each patty and let it melt.
4. While the burger patties are cooking, lightly toast the hamburger buns on the grill or in a toaster.
5. To assemble the Tillamook cheeseburgers, place a lettuce leaf on the bottom half of each toasted bun, followed by a cooked burger patty with melted Tillamook cheese.
6. Top the burger patties with sliced tomatoes, sliced red onions, and pickles.

7. If desired, spread ketchup, mustard, or mayonnaise on the top half of each toasted bun before placing it on top of the assembled burgers.
8. Serve the Tillamook cheeseburgers immediately, accompanied by your favorite side dishes such as French fries, potato chips, or a crisp green salad.
9. Enjoy the delicious combination of juicy burger patties, melted Tillamook cheddar cheese, and fresh toppings in every bite of this classic cheeseburger.

These Tillamook cheeseburgers are perfect for grilling season, backyard barbecues, or casual weeknight dinners. With the rich and creamy flavor of Tillamook cheese, they're sure to be a hit with family and friends alike!

Oregon Trail Mix Cookies

Ingredients:

- 1/2 cup unsalted butter, softened
- 1/2 cup granulated sugar
- 1/2 cup brown sugar, packed
- 1 large egg
- 1 teaspoon vanilla extract
- 1 cup all-purpose flour
- 1/2 teaspoon baking soda
- 1/4 teaspoon salt
- 1 cup old-fashioned rolled oats
- 1/2 cup chopped Oregon hazelnuts
- 1/2 cup dried cranberries
- 1/2 cup chocolate chips or chunks

Instructions:

1. Preheat your oven to 350°F (175°C). Line a baking sheet with parchment paper or silicone baking mat.
2. In a large mixing bowl, cream together the softened butter, granulated sugar, and brown sugar until light and fluffy.
3. Beat in the egg and vanilla extract until well combined.
4. In a separate bowl, whisk together the all-purpose flour, baking soda, and salt.
5. Gradually add the dry ingredients to the wet ingredients, mixing until just combined.
6. Stir in the rolled oats, chopped Oregon hazelnuts, dried cranberries, and chocolate chips until evenly distributed throughout the cookie dough.
7. Using a spoon or cookie scoop, drop rounded tablespoons of dough onto the prepared baking sheet, spacing them about 2 inches apart.
8. Gently flatten each cookie dough ball with the back of a spoon or your fingers to form a thick disc.
9. Bake the cookies in the preheated oven for 10-12 minutes, or until the edges are golden brown and the centers are set.
10. Remove the cookies from the oven and let them cool on the baking sheet for a few minutes before transferring them to a wire rack to cool completely.
11. Once cooled, serve and enjoy these delicious Oregon Trail Mix Cookies as a tasty snack or dessert.

12. Store any leftover cookies in an airtight container at room temperature for up to one week.

These Oregon Trail Mix Cookies are perfect for enjoying on the go, packing in lunchboxes, or sharing with friends and family. With their hearty oats, crunchy hazelnuts, sweet cranberries, and decadent chocolate, they're a delightful combination of flavors and textures that everyone will love!

Hazelnut Chocolate Bark

Ingredients:

- 10 ounces (about 2 cups) semi-sweet or dark chocolate chips
- 1 cup Oregon hazelnuts, toasted and roughly chopped
- Sea salt flakes (optional, for garnish)

Instructions:

1. Preheat your oven to 350°F (175°C). Spread the hazelnuts in a single layer on a baking sheet and toast them in the preheated oven for 10-12 minutes, or until fragrant and golden brown. Keep an eye on them to prevent burning. Once toasted, remove the hazelnuts from the oven and let them cool slightly. Once cool enough to handle, rub the hazelnuts between your hands or in a clean kitchen towel to remove the skins. Roughly chop the hazelnuts and set aside.
2. Line a baking sheet with parchment paper or a silicone baking mat and set aside.
3. In a heatproof bowl set over a pot of simmering water (double boiler), melt the chocolate chips, stirring occasionally with a spatula, until smooth and completely melted.
4. Once the chocolate is melted, remove the bowl from the heat and stir in 3/4 cup of the toasted chopped hazelnuts, reserving the remaining 1/4 cup for garnish.
5. Pour the melted chocolate mixture onto the prepared baking sheet and use a spatula to spread it out into an even layer, about 1/4 to 1/2 inch thick.
6. Sprinkle the reserved chopped hazelnuts evenly over the melted chocolate, gently pressing them down into the chocolate.
7. If desired, sprinkle a pinch of sea salt flakes over the top of the chocolate bark for a delicious contrast of flavors.
8. Place the baking sheet in the refrigerator for about 30 minutes, or until the chocolate is firm and set.
9. Once the chocolate bark is set, remove it from the refrigerator and use a sharp knife to break it into pieces or cut it into squares.
10. Serve the hazelnut chocolate bark immediately, or store it in an airtight container in the refrigerator for up to two weeks.

Enjoy this delicious hazelnut chocolate bark as a sweet treat or give it as a homemade gift to friends and family. With its rich chocolate flavor and crunchy hazelnuts, it's sure to be a hit with everyone who tries it!

Tillamook Cheese Fondue

Ingredients:

- 1 garlic clove, halved
- 1 cup dry white wine
- 1 tablespoon lemon juice
- 8 ounces Tillamook medium cheddar cheese, shredded
- 8 ounces Tillamook sharp cheddar cheese, shredded
- 1 tablespoon cornstarch
- 1 tablespoon water
- 1/4 teaspoon ground black pepper
- Pinch of nutmeg (optional)
- Assorted dippers (such as cubed bread, blanched vegetables, cooked sausage or ham)

Instructions:

1. Rub the inside of a fondue pot or heavy-bottomed saucepan with the cut side of the garlic clove, then discard the garlic.
2. In the fondue pot or saucepan, combine the dry white wine and lemon juice. Heat over medium heat until hot but not boiling.
3. In a small bowl, dissolve the cornstarch in the water to make a slurry.
4. Gradually add the shredded Tillamook medium cheddar cheese and Tillamook sharp cheddar cheese to the hot wine mixture, stirring constantly with a wooden spoon until the cheese is melted and the mixture is smooth.
5. Stir in the cornstarch slurry and continue to cook, stirring constantly, until the fondue is thickened and glossy.
6. Season the fondue with ground black pepper and a pinch of nutmeg, if desired, for added flavor.
7. Transfer the fondue pot to a fondue burner or keep it warm over low heat on the stove.
8. Serve the Tillamook Cheese Fondue immediately with assorted dippers for dipping.
9. Enjoy the creamy and flavorful Tillamook Cheese Fondue with your favorite dippers, such as cubed bread, blanched vegetables, or cooked sausage or ham.
10. Stir the fondue occasionally to prevent it from becoming too thick or sticking to the bottom of the pot.

11. If the fondue becomes too thick, you can thin it out with a little more wine or lemon juice.
12. Dip, dunk, and savor every bite of this delicious Tillamook Cheese Fondue for a cozy and satisfying dining experience!

Oregon Berry Parfait

Ingredients:

- 2 cups mixed Oregon berries (such as strawberries, raspberries, blueberries, blackberries)
- 2 cups Greek yogurt or vanilla yogurt
- 1/4 cup honey or maple syrup (optional, for sweetening)
- 1 cup granola or toasted oats
- Fresh mint leaves for garnish (optional)

Instructions:

1. Rinse the mixed Oregon berries under cold water and drain them well. Remove any stems or leaves and pat them dry with paper towels.
2. If using Greek yogurt, you may want to sweeten it with honey or maple syrup to taste. Stir the honey or maple syrup into the yogurt until well combined.
3. In serving glasses or bowls, layer the Greek yogurt, mixed Oregon berries, and granola in alternating layers.
4. Start by spooning a layer of yogurt into the bottom of each glass or bowl, followed by a layer of mixed berries, and then a layer of granola. Repeat the layers until the glasses or bowls are filled, finishing with a final layer of yogurt on top.
5. Garnish each parfait with a few fresh berries and mint leaves for a pop of color and freshness, if desired.
6. Serve the Oregon Berry Parfaits immediately as a delicious and nutritious dessert or snack.
7. Enjoy the vibrant flavors and textures of the mixed Oregon berries, creamy yogurt, and crunchy granola in every spoonful of this delightful parfait!

These Oregon Berry Parfaits are perfect for serving at breakfast, brunch, or as a light and refreshing dessert after a meal. They're not only delicious and satisfying but also packed with vitamins, antioxidants, and fiber from the fresh berries, making them a healthy treat that everyone will love.

Hazelnut Espresso Brownies

Ingredients:

- 1/2 cup (1 stick) unsalted butter
- 1 cup granulated sugar
- 2 large eggs
- 1 teaspoon vanilla extract
- 1/2 cup all-purpose flour
- 1/3 cup unsweetened cocoa powder
- 1/4 teaspoon salt
- 2 tablespoons espresso powder
- 1/2 cup chopped Oregon hazelnuts
- 1/2 cup semi-sweet chocolate chips or chunks

Instructions:

1. Preheat your oven to 350°F (175°C). Grease or line an 8x8-inch baking pan with parchment paper, leaving some overhang for easy removal.
2. In a medium saucepan, melt the butter over low heat. Once melted, remove from heat and let cool slightly.
3. Stir in the granulated sugar until well combined.
4. Beat in the eggs, one at a time, until incorporated.
5. Stir in the vanilla extract.
6. In a separate bowl, sift together the all-purpose flour, cocoa powder, salt, and espresso powder.
7. Gradually add the dry ingredients to the wet ingredients, mixing until just combined.
8. Fold in the chopped Oregon hazelnuts and semi-sweet chocolate chips or chunks until evenly distributed throughout the batter.
9. Pour the batter into the prepared baking pan and spread it out evenly with a spatula.
10. Bake in the preheated oven for 25-30 minutes, or until a toothpick inserted into the center comes out with a few moist crumbs.
11. Remove the brownies from the oven and let them cool completely in the pan on a wire rack.
12. Once cooled, lift the brownies out of the pan using the parchment paper overhang and transfer them to a cutting board.

13. Cut the brownies into squares or rectangles and serve.
14. Enjoy these decadent hazelnut espresso brownies with a glass of milk, a cup of coffee, or on their own as a delicious treat!

These hazelnut espresso brownies are rich, fudgy, and packed with flavor. The combination of chocolate, hazelnuts, and espresso creates a truly irresistible indulgence that's perfect for satisfying your sweet cravings.

Tillamook Yogurt Dip

Ingredients:

- 1 cup Tillamook plain yogurt
- 1/4 cup mayonnaise
- 2 tablespoons chopped fresh herbs (such as dill, parsley, chives)
- 1 tablespoon lemon juice
- 1 teaspoon garlic powder
- 1/2 teaspoon onion powder
- Salt and pepper to taste

Instructions:

1. In a medium mixing bowl, combine the Tillamook plain yogurt, mayonnaise, chopped fresh herbs, lemon juice, garlic powder, and onion powder. Mix well until smooth and creamy.
2. Season the dip with salt and pepper to taste, adjusting the seasoning as needed.
3. Cover the bowl with plastic wrap or transfer the dip to an airtight container.
4. Refrigerate the Tillamook yogurt dip for at least 1 hour to allow the flavors to meld and the dip to chill.
5. Before serving, give the dip a quick stir and taste for seasoning, adding more salt and pepper if necessary.
6. Serve the Tillamook yogurt dip with your favorite dippers, such as potato chips, tortilla chips, pretzels, carrot sticks, celery sticks, cucumber slices, or bell pepper strips.
7. Enjoy the creamy and flavorful Tillamook yogurt dip as a delicious snack, appetizer, or condiment for sandwiches and wraps.

This homemade Tillamook yogurt dip is versatile, customizable, and perfect for any occasion. Whether you're hosting a party, enjoying a movie night at home, or packing a picnic, this creamy dip is sure to be a hit with everyone!

Oregon Pear and Hazelnut Salad

Ingredients:

For the salad:

- 4 cups mixed salad greens (such as arugula, spinach, and romaine lettuce)
- 2 ripe Oregon pears, thinly sliced
- 1/2 cup Oregon hazelnuts, toasted and roughly chopped
- 1/4 cup crumbled blue cheese or goat cheese (optional)
- 1/4 cup dried cranberries or cherries (optional)

For the vinaigrette:

- 1/4 cup extra virgin olive oil
- 2 tablespoons balsamic vinegar
- 1 tablespoon honey or maple syrup
- 1 teaspoon Dijon mustard
- Salt and pepper to taste

Instructions:

1. In a small bowl, whisk together the extra virgin olive oil, balsamic vinegar, honey or maple syrup, Dijon mustard, salt, and pepper to make the vinaigrette. Set aside.
2. In a large salad bowl, combine the mixed salad greens, thinly sliced Oregon pears, toasted and chopped Oregon hazelnuts, crumbled blue cheese or goat cheese (if using), and dried cranberries or cherries (if using).
3. Drizzle the vinaigrette over the salad ingredients, tossing gently to coat everything evenly.
4. Taste the salad and adjust the seasoning as needed, adding more salt and pepper if necessary.
5. Serve the Oregon Pear and Hazelnut Salad immediately as a refreshing appetizer or side dish.
6. Enjoy the crisp and juicy Oregon pears, crunchy toasted hazelnuts, and tangy vinaigrette in every bite of this delicious salad!

This Oregon Pear and Hazelnut Salad is perfect for any occasion, from casual weeknight dinners to elegant dinner parties. It's a wonderful way to showcase the seasonal flavors of the Pacific Northwest and add a touch of freshness to your meal.

Marionberry Sorbet

Ingredients:

- 4 cups fresh or frozen marionberries
- 1 cup granulated sugar
- 1/4 cup water
- 2 tablespoons freshly squeezed lemon juice
- 1 tablespoon vodka (optional, to prevent sorbet from freezing too hard)

Instructions:

1. In a small saucepan, combine the granulated sugar and water over medium heat. Stir until the sugar is dissolved, and the mixture comes to a gentle simmer.
2. Remove the sugar syrup from the heat and let it cool completely.
3. In a blender or food processor, puree the marionberries until smooth. Strain the puree through a fine-mesh sieve to remove the seeds, if desired.
4. In a large bowl, combine the strained marionberry puree with the cooled sugar syrup and freshly squeezed lemon juice. Stir until well combined.
5. If using vodka, stir it into the marionberry mixture. The alcohol will help prevent the sorbet from freezing too hard.
6. Pour the marionberry mixture into an ice cream maker and churn according to the manufacturer's instructions until it reaches a thick and creamy consistency.
7. Transfer the churned sorbet to a freezer-safe container and freeze for at least 4 hours or until firm.
8. Before serving, let the marionberry sorbet sit at room temperature for a few minutes to soften slightly. Scoop into bowls or cones and enjoy!
9. Garnish the marionberry sorbet with fresh marionberries, mint leaves, or a sprinkle of powdered sugar, if desired.
10. Store any leftover sorbet in the freezer in an airtight container for up to 2 weeks.
11. Enjoy the refreshing and fruity flavor of marionberry sorbet as a delightful dessert on a hot summer day or anytime you crave a sweet and tangy treat!

This marionberry sorbet is bursting with the natural sweetness and vibrant color of marionberries, making it a perfect dessert for showcasing the flavors of the Pacific Northwest.

Hazelnut Crusted Tilapia

Ingredients:

- 4 tilapia fillets
- 1 cup Oregon hazelnuts, toasted and finely chopped
- 1/2 cup breadcrumbs
- 1/4 cup all-purpose flour
- 2 eggs, beaten
- Salt and pepper to taste
- Olive oil or cooking spray for baking

Instructions:

1. Preheat your oven to 400°F (200°C). Line a baking sheet with parchment paper or lightly grease it with olive oil or cooking spray.
2. In a shallow dish, combine the finely chopped hazelnuts, breadcrumbs, and a pinch of salt and pepper. Mix well to combine.
3. Place the all-purpose flour in another shallow dish.
4. Season the tilapia fillets with salt and pepper on both sides.
5. Dredge each tilapia fillet in the all-purpose flour, shaking off any excess.
6. Dip the floured tilapia fillets into the beaten eggs, allowing any excess egg to drip off.
7. Press the egg-coated tilapia fillets into the hazelnut and breadcrumb mixture, coating them evenly on both sides. Press gently to adhere the coating to the fish.
8. Place the coated tilapia fillets onto the prepared baking sheet.
9. Lightly spray the tops of the coated tilapia fillets with olive oil or cooking spray to help them brown and crisp up in the oven.
10. Bake the hazelnut crusted tilapia fillets in the preheated oven for 12-15 minutes, or until the fish is cooked through and the coating is golden brown and crispy.
11. Remove the tilapia fillets from the oven and let them rest for a few minutes before serving.
12. Serve the hazelnut crusted tilapia fillets hot, garnished with fresh herbs or lemon wedges if desired.
13. Enjoy the delicious combination of tender tilapia and crunchy hazelnut crust in every bite of this flavorful seafood dish!

Hazelnut crusted tilapia is perfect for a quick and easy weeknight dinner or a special occasion meal. Serve it with your favorite side dishes, such as roasted vegetables, rice, or a fresh green salad, for a complete and satisfying meal.

Tillamook Cheese Stuffed Mushrooms

Ingredients:

- 16 large button mushrooms
- 8 ounces cream cheese, softened
- 1 cup shredded Tillamook cheddar cheese
- 2 cloves garlic, minced
- 2 tablespoons chopped fresh parsley
- Salt and pepper to taste
- Olive oil or cooking spray, for greasing
- Optional: grated Parmesan cheese for topping

Instructions:

1. Preheat your oven to 375°F (190°C). Grease a baking sheet with olive oil or cooking spray.
2. Clean the mushrooms and remove the stems. Set aside the mushroom caps and chop the stems finely.
3. In a mixing bowl, combine the softened cream cheese, shredded Tillamook cheddar cheese, minced garlic, chopped parsley, and chopped mushroom stems. Season with salt and pepper to taste.
4. Stuff each mushroom cap with a generous amount of the cheese mixture, pressing it down slightly to ensure it fills the cavity.
5. Place the stuffed mushrooms on the prepared baking sheet.
6. Optional: Sprinkle grated Parmesan cheese over the stuffed mushrooms for an extra cheesy topping.
7. Bake in the preheated oven for 15-20 minutes, or until the mushrooms are tender and the cheese is melted and golden brown on top.
8. Remove from the oven and let cool slightly before serving.
9. Garnish with additional chopped parsley if desired, and serve warm.

These Tillamook cheese stuffed mushrooms are sure to be a hit at any party or gathering. Enjoy the creamy, cheesy goodness in every bite!

Oregon Berry Crisp

Ingredients:

For the berry filling:

- 4 cups mixed Oregon berries (such as strawberries, blueberries, blackberries, raspberries)
- 1/4 cup granulated sugar
- 2 tablespoons all-purpose flour
- 1 tablespoon freshly squeezed lemon juice
- 1 teaspoon vanilla extract

For the crisp topping:

- 1 cup old-fashioned rolled oats
- 1/2 cup all-purpose flour
- 1/2 cup packed brown sugar
- 1/2 teaspoon ground cinnamon
- 1/4 teaspoon salt
- 1/2 cup unsalted butter, melted

Instructions:

1. Preheat your oven to 375°F (190°C). Grease a 9x9-inch baking dish with butter or non-stick cooking spray.
2. In a large mixing bowl, combine the mixed Oregon berries, granulated sugar, all-purpose flour, lemon juice, and vanilla extract. Toss gently until the berries are evenly coated with the sugar mixture.
3. Transfer the berry mixture to the prepared baking dish, spreading it out into an even layer.
4. In another mixing bowl, combine the old-fashioned rolled oats, all-purpose flour, brown sugar, ground cinnamon, and salt for the crisp topping. Mix until well combined.
5. Pour the melted unsalted butter over the oat mixture and stir until the ingredients are evenly moistened and clump together.
6. Sprinkle the crisp topping evenly over the berry filling in the baking dish.

7. Bake the Oregon Berry Crisp in the preheated oven for 35-40 minutes, or until the topping is golden brown and the berry filling is bubbly around the edges.
8. Remove the crisp from the oven and let it cool for a few minutes before serving.
9. Serve the Oregon Berry Crisp warm, either on its own or topped with a scoop of vanilla ice cream or a dollop of whipped cream.
10. Enjoy the irresistible combination of sweet, juicy berries and crunchy oat topping in this delicious Pacific Northwest-inspired dessert!

This Oregon Berry Crisp is perfect for showcasing the vibrant flavors of fresh berries and makes a delightful treat for any occasion, from casual weeknight dinners to special celebrations with family and friends.

Hazelnut Encrusted Brie

Ingredients:

- 1 wheel of Brie cheese (about 8-12 ounces)
- 1 cup Oregon hazelnuts, toasted and finely chopped
- 1/4 cup all-purpose flour
- 2 large eggs, beaten
- 1 tablespoon water
- Salt and pepper to taste
- Olive oil or cooking spray, for greasing

Optional toppings:

- Honey
- Fig jam or preserves
- Fresh herbs (such as rosemary or thyme)

Instructions:

1. Preheat your oven to 375°F (190°C). Grease a baking sheet with olive oil or cooking spray.
2. Remove the outer rind from the Brie cheese, if desired. Some people prefer to leave it on for added flavor and texture, while others prefer to remove it for a smoother texture.
3. In a shallow dish, combine the finely chopped hazelnuts with a pinch of salt and pepper.
4. In another shallow dish, place the all-purpose flour.
5. In a third shallow dish, whisk together the beaten eggs and water to create an egg wash.
6. Dredge the Brie cheese wheel in the all-purpose flour, shaking off any excess.
7. Dip the floured Brie cheese in the egg wash, ensuring that it is coated on all sides.
8. Roll the coated Brie cheese in the chopped hazelnuts, pressing gently to adhere the nuts to the cheese and ensuring that it is evenly coated.
9. Place the hazelnut-encrusted Brie cheese on the prepared baking sheet.
10. Bake in the preheated oven for 10-15 minutes, or until the cheese is soft and gooey and the hazelnut crust is golden brown and crispy.

11. Remove from the oven and let the hazelnut-encrusted Brie cheese cool for a few minutes before serving.
12. Optional: Drizzle honey over the warm hazelnut-encrusted Brie cheese for added sweetness, or serve it with fig jam or preserves for a delicious pairing.
13. Garnish with fresh herbs, if desired, for a pop of color and flavor.
14. Serve the hazelnut-encrusted Brie cheese warm, either on its own or with crackers, bread, or sliced fruit for dipping.

Enjoy the creamy, nutty goodness of hazelnut-encrusted Brie cheese as a delightful appetizer or party snack that's sure to impress your guests!

Tillamook Cheese and Herb Bread

Ingredients:

- 3 cups all-purpose flour
- 1 tablespoon baking powder
- 1 teaspoon salt
- 1/4 teaspoon baking soda
- 1/2 cup unsalted butter, chilled and cubed
- 1 cup shredded Tillamook cheddar cheese
- 2 tablespoons chopped fresh herbs (such as parsley, chives, or thyme)
- 1 cup buttermilk

Instructions:

1. Preheat your oven to 375°F (190°C). Grease a 9x5-inch loaf pan or line it with parchment paper.
2. In a large mixing bowl, whisk together the all-purpose flour, baking powder, salt, and baking soda.
3. Add the chilled and cubed unsalted butter to the flour mixture. Use a pastry cutter or your fingers to cut the butter into the flour until the mixture resembles coarse crumbs.
4. Stir in the shredded Tillamook cheddar cheese and chopped fresh herbs until evenly distributed.
5. Make a well in the center of the flour mixture and pour in the buttermilk. Use a wooden spoon or rubber spatula to gently mix until the dough comes together. Be careful not to overmix.
6. Transfer the dough to the prepared loaf pan and use a spatula or your hands to spread it out evenly.
7. Bake in the preheated oven for 40-45 minutes, or until the top is golden brown and a toothpick inserted into the center comes out clean.
8. Remove the bread from the oven and let it cool in the pan for 10 minutes before transferring it to a wire rack to cool completely.
9. Once cooled, slice the Tillamook cheese and herb bread and serve.

Enjoy the delicious flavor of Tillamook cheese and fresh herbs in every bite of this savory bread! It's perfect for enjoying with your favorite meals or as a tasty snack any time of day.

Oregon Berry Pie

Ingredients:

For the pie crust:

- 2 1/2 cups all-purpose flour
- 1 teaspoon salt
- 1 tablespoon granulated sugar
- 1 cup (2 sticks) cold unsalted butter, cubed
- 6-8 tablespoons ice water

For the berry filling:

- 5 cups mixed Oregon berries (such as strawberries, blueberries, blackberries, raspberries)
- 3/4 cup granulated sugar
- 1/4 cup cornstarch
- 1 tablespoon freshly squeezed lemon juice
- 1 teaspoon vanilla extract
- 1 tablespoon unsalted butter, diced

For egg wash:

- 1 large egg
- 1 tablespoon water

Instructions:

1. Prepare the pie crust:
    - In a large mixing bowl, whisk together the all-purpose flour, salt, and granulated sugar.
    - Add the cubed cold unsalted butter to the flour mixture. Use a pastry cutter or your fingers to cut the butter into the flour until the mixture resembles coarse crumbs.
    - Gradually add the ice water, 1 tablespoon at a time, mixing with a fork until the dough comes together. Be careful not to overmix.

- Divide the dough into two equal portions, shape each into a disc, wrap in plastic wrap, and refrigerate for at least 1 hour.
2. Preheat your oven to 375°F (190°C). Place a baking sheet on the middle rack to catch any drips from the pie.
3. Prepare the berry filling:
    - In a large mixing bowl, combine the mixed Oregon berries, granulated sugar, cornstarch, lemon juice, and vanilla extract. Gently toss until the berries are coated evenly.
4. Roll out one disc of chilled pie dough on a lightly floured surface into a circle about 12 inches in diameter. Carefully transfer the rolled-out dough to a 9-inch pie dish, gently pressing it into the bottom and up the sides.
5. Pour the berry filling into the prepared pie crust, spreading it out evenly. Dot the top of the filling with diced unsalted butter.
6. Roll out the second disc of chilled pie dough into a circle about 12 inches in diameter. Place it over the filled pie. Trim any excess dough and crimp the edges to seal. Cut a few slits in the top crust to allow steam to escape during baking.
7. In a small bowl, whisk together the egg and water to make the egg wash. Brush the top crust with the egg wash.
8. Place the pie on the preheated baking sheet in the oven and bake for 50-60 minutes, or until the crust is golden brown and the filling is bubbling.
9. Remove the pie from the oven and let it cool on a wire rack for at least 2 hours before slicing and serving.
10. Serve slices of Oregon berry pie on their own or with a scoop of vanilla ice cream or a dollop of whipped cream for a delicious dessert treat!

Enjoy the burst of flavor from the mixed Oregon berries in every bite of this homemade pie, a perfect way to celebrate the bounty of the Pacific Northwest!

Hazelnut Pancakes

Ingredients:

- 1 cup all-purpose flour
- 2 tablespoons granulated sugar
- 1 teaspoon baking powder
- 1/2 teaspoon baking soda
- 1/4 teaspoon salt
- 1 cup buttermilk
- 1 large egg
- 2 tablespoons unsalted butter, melted
- 1/2 teaspoon vanilla extract
- 1/2 cup Oregon hazelnuts, toasted and finely chopped
- Butter or cooking spray, for greasing the griddle or skillet
- Maple syrup or your favorite pancake toppings, for serving

Instructions:

1. In a large mixing bowl, whisk together the all-purpose flour, granulated sugar, baking powder, baking soda, and salt until well combined.
2. In a separate mixing bowl, whisk together the buttermilk, egg, melted unsalted butter, and vanilla extract until smooth.
3. Pour the wet ingredients into the dry ingredients and stir until just combined. Do not overmix. It's okay if the batter is slightly lumpy.
4. Gently fold in the toasted and finely chopped Oregon hazelnuts until evenly distributed throughout the batter.
5. Preheat a griddle or skillet over medium heat. Lightly grease the cooking surface with butter or cooking spray.
6. Pour about 1/4 cup of batter onto the hot griddle or skillet for each pancake. Use the back of a spoon or a spatula to spread the batter into a round shape if necessary.
7. Cook the pancakes for 2-3 minutes, or until bubbles form on the surface and the edges begin to look set.
8. Flip the pancakes and cook for an additional 1-2 minutes, or until golden brown and cooked through.
9. Transfer the cooked hazelnut pancakes to a plate and keep warm while you cook the remaining pancakes.

10. Serve the hazelnut pancakes hot, topped with maple syrup or your favorite pancake toppings, such as fresh berries, sliced bananas, whipped cream, or a dusting of powdered sugar.
11. Enjoy the nutty flavor and crunchy texture of these delicious hazelnut pancakes as a delightful breakfast or brunch treat!

These hazelnut pancakes are sure to be a hit with the whole family. They're perfect for special occasions or any day when you're craving a comforting and indulgent breakfast.

Tillamook Cheese Soup

Ingredients:

- 4 tablespoons unsalted butter
- 1/4 cup all-purpose flour
- 4 cups chicken or vegetable broth
- 2 cups milk
- 2 cups shredded Tillamook cheddar cheese
- 1 cup shredded Tillamook pepper jack cheese
- 1 cup shredded Tillamook medium cheddar cheese
- 1/2 teaspoon garlic powder
- 1/2 teaspoon onion powder
- Salt and pepper to taste
- Optional toppings: crumbled cooked bacon, chopped green onions, diced tomatoes, sour cream

Instructions:

1. In a large pot or Dutch oven, melt the unsalted butter over medium heat.
2. Once the butter is melted, add the all-purpose flour to the pot and whisk continuously to form a roux. Cook the roux for 2-3 minutes, stirring constantly, until it turns golden brown and has a nutty aroma.
3. Gradually pour in the chicken or vegetable broth while whisking continuously to prevent lumps from forming.
4. Stir in the milk, garlic powder, and onion powder until well combined. Bring the soup to a simmer, then reduce the heat to low.
5. Add the shredded Tillamook cheddar cheese, Tillamook pepper jack cheese, and Tillamook medium cheddar cheese to the pot, stirring constantly until the cheese is melted and the soup is smooth and creamy.
6. Season the soup with salt and pepper to taste, adjusting the seasoning as needed.
7. Continue to simmer the soup for an additional 5-10 minutes, stirring occasionally, to allow the flavors to meld together.
8. Once the soup is heated through and well blended, remove it from the heat.
9. Ladle the Tillamook cheese soup into bowls and garnish with optional toppings such as crumbled cooked bacon, chopped green onions, diced tomatoes, or sour cream.

10. Serve the soup hot and enjoy the creamy and cheesy goodness of Tillamook cheese in every spoonful!

This Tillamook cheese soup is perfect for warming up on a cold day or for enjoying as a comforting meal any time of the year. Serve it with crusty bread or a side salad for a complete and satisfying dish.

Oregon Berry Salsa

Ingredients:

- 1 cup mixed Oregon berries (such as strawberries, blueberries, blackberries, raspberries), chopped
- 1/2 red onion, finely chopped
- 1 jalapeño pepper, seeds removed and finely chopped
- 1/4 cup fresh cilantro, chopped
- 1 tablespoon freshly squeezed lime juice
- 1 tablespoon honey or maple syrup
- Salt and pepper to taste

Instructions:

1. In a medium mixing bowl, combine the chopped mixed Oregon berries, finely chopped red onion, finely chopped jalapeño pepper, and chopped fresh cilantro.
2. Drizzle the freshly squeezed lime juice and honey or maple syrup over the berry mixture.
3. Season with salt and pepper to taste, adjusting the seasoning as needed.
4. Gently toss the ingredients together until well combined.
5. Cover the bowl with plastic wrap and refrigerate the Oregon berry salsa for at least 30 minutes to allow the flavors to meld together.
6. Before serving, give the salsa a quick stir and taste for seasoning, adding more salt, pepper, lime juice, or honey/maple syrup if desired.
7. Serve the Oregon berry salsa as a dip with tortilla chips, or use it as a topping for grilled fish, chicken, or tacos.
8. Enjoy the vibrant colors and fresh flavors of this delightful salsa, highlighting the delicious bounty of Oregon berries!

This Oregon berry salsa is perfect for summer gatherings, picnics, or as a healthy snack any time of the year. It's versatile, customizable, and sure to be a hit with friends and family alike!

Hazelnut Crusted Tofu

Ingredients:

- 1 block (14-16 ounces) extra-firm tofu
- 1 cup Oregon hazelnuts, toasted and finely chopped
- 1/2 cup breadcrumbs (panko or regular)
- 1/4 cup all-purpose flour
- 1 teaspoon garlic powder
- 1 teaspoon paprika
- 1/2 teaspoon salt
- 1/4 teaspoon black pepper
- 2 large eggs, beaten (for vegan option, substitute with plant-based milk or aquafaba)
- Olive oil or cooking spray, for greasing

Instructions:

1. Preheat your oven to 400°F (200°C). Grease a baking sheet with olive oil or cooking spray.
2. Drain the block of tofu and pat it dry with paper towels to remove excess moisture. Slice the tofu into 1/2-inch thick slices, then cut each slice into smaller pieces (such as rectangles or triangles).
3. In a shallow dish, combine the finely chopped Oregon hazelnuts, breadcrumbs, all-purpose flour, garlic powder, paprika, salt, and black pepper. Mix well to combine.
4. Dip each tofu piece into the beaten eggs (or plant-based milk or aquafaba), shaking off any excess liquid.
5. Press the egg-coated tofu pieces into the hazelnut and breadcrumb mixture, coating them evenly on all sides. Press gently to adhere the coating to the tofu.
6. Place the coated tofu pieces on the prepared baking sheet in a single layer, leaving some space between each piece.
7. Drizzle or spray a little olive oil over the top of the coated tofu pieces to help them brown and crisp up in the oven.
8. Bake the hazelnut-crusted tofu in the preheated oven for 20-25 minutes, or until the coating is golden brown and crispy, and the tofu is heated through.
9. Remove the tofu from the oven and let it cool slightly before serving.
10. Serve the hazelnut-crusted tofu hot as a main dish or appetizer, accompanied by your favorite dipping sauce or alongside a salad or grain dish.

11. Enjoy the crunchy texture and nutty flavor of this delicious hazelnut-crusted tofu, perfect for a vegetarian meal or as a tasty protein option for any occasion!

This hazelnut-crusted tofu is versatile and can be enjoyed in sandwiches, wraps, stir-fries, or any dish where you'd use traditional breaded tofu. It's a nutritious and flavorful alternative that's sure to please your taste buds.

Tillamook Ice Cream Sandwiches

Ingredients:

- Tillamook ice cream (your favorite flavor)
- Cookies of your choice (homemade or store-bought)

Instructions:

1. Let the Tillamook ice cream soften slightly at room temperature until it's easy to scoop but not melted.
2. Line a baking sheet or tray with parchment paper.
3. Take one cookie and place a scoop of Tillamook ice cream on the flat side of the cookie.
4. Place another cookie on top of the ice cream scoop, pressing down gently to create a sandwich.
5. Use a spatula or the back of a spoon to smooth the edges of the ice cream sandwich, if needed.
6. Repeat the process with the remaining cookies and ice cream until you have made as many sandwiches as desired.
7. Place the assembled ice cream sandwiches on the prepared baking sheet or tray.
8. If desired, you can roll the edges of the ice cream sandwiches in sprinkles, chopped nuts, or mini chocolate chips for added texture and flavor.
9. Once all the ice cream sandwiches are assembled, transfer the baking sheet or tray to the freezer.
10. Allow the ice cream sandwiches to freeze for at least 1-2 hours, or until the ice cream is firm.
11. Once frozen, remove the ice cream sandwiches from the freezer and serve immediately.
12. Enjoy these homemade Tillamook ice cream sandwiches as a delicious and refreshing treat on a hot day or any time you're craving something sweet!

Feel free to get creative with your ice cream sandwich combinations by using different flavors of Tillamook ice cream and various types of cookies. Whether you prefer classic chocolate chip cookies, oatmeal cookies, or even brownie cookies, there's no wrong way to enjoy these delightful frozen treats!

Ingredients:

- Tillamook ice cream (your favorite flavor)
- Cookies of your choice (homemade or store-bought)

Instructions:

1. Let the Tillamook ice cream soften slightly at room temperature until it's easy to scoop but not melted.
2. Line a baking sheet or tray with parchment paper.
3. Take one cookie and place a scoop of Tillamook ice cream on the flat side of the cookie.
4. Place another cookie on top of the ice cream scoop, pressing down gently to create a sandwich.
5. Use a spatula or the back of a spoon to smooth the edges of the ice cream sandwich, if needed.
6. Repeat the process with the remaining cookies and ice cream until you have made as many sandwiches as desired.
7. Place the assembled ice cream sandwiches on the prepared baking sheet or tray.
8. If desired, you can roll the edges of the ice cream sandwiches in sprinkles, chopped nuts, or mini chocolate chips for added texture and flavor.
9. Once all the ice cream sandwiches are assembled, transfer the baking sheet or tray to the freezer.
10. Allow the ice cream sandwiches to freeze for at least 1-2 hours, or until the ice cream is firm.
11. Once frozen, remove the ice cream sandwiches from the freezer and serve immediately.
12. Enjoy these homemade Tillamook ice cream sandwiches as a delicious and refreshing treat on a hot day or any time you're craving something sweet!

Feel free to get creative with your ice cream sandwich combinations by using different flavors of Tillamook ice cream and various types of cookies. Whether you prefer classic chocolate chip cookies, oatmeal cookies, or even brownie cookies, there's no wrong way to enjoy these delightful frozen treats!

Oregon Berry Lemonade

Ingredients:

- 1 cup mixed Oregon berries (such as strawberries, blueberries, blackberries, raspberries)
- 1 cup granulated sugar
- 1 cup freshly squeezed lemon juice (about 4-6 lemons)
- 4 cups cold water
- Ice cubes
- Fresh mint leaves for garnish (optional)

Instructions:

1. In a small saucepan, combine the mixed Oregon berries and granulated sugar. Heat over medium-low heat, stirring occasionally, until the sugar has dissolved and the berries have softened, about 5-7 minutes. Remove from heat and let cool slightly.
2. Once the berry mixture has cooled slightly, use a fine mesh sieve or cheesecloth to strain the mixture, pressing down with a spoon to extract as much juice as possible. Discard the solids and set the berry syrup aside.
3. In a large pitcher, combine the freshly squeezed lemon juice and cold water.
4. Stir in the berry syrup until well combined, adjusting the sweetness to taste by adding more sugar if desired.
5. Fill glasses with ice cubes and pour the Oregon berry lemonade over the ice.
6. Garnish with fresh mint leaves, if desired, for a pop of color and added freshness.
7. Stir the lemonade gently before serving to distribute the flavors evenly.
8. Serve the Oregon berry lemonade immediately and enjoy its refreshing and fruity flavor on a hot day!

Feel free to customize this Oregon berry lemonade recipe to suit your taste preferences. You can adjust the sweetness by adding more or less sugar, or you can experiment with different combinations of Oregon berries for unique flavor variations. Cheers to a delicious and refreshing homemade lemonade!

www.ingramcontent.com/pod-product-compliance
Lightning Source LLC
LaVergne TN
LVHW081608060526
838201LV00054B/2146